I0126463

WEANING

YOUR

GOAT KIDS

A SIMPLE GUIDE

Felicity McCullough

Paperback Edition

My Lap Shop Publishers

Plymouth, England

www.mylapshop.com

ISBN: 978-1-78165-043-1

Series: Goat Knowledge 8

Disclaimer

This book is meant to be STRICTLY AN EDUCATIONAL AND INFORMATIONAL TOOL ONLY. The suggestions contained in this material might not be suitable for everyone. It is not intended to provide diagnosis or treatment. The author obtained the information from sources believed to be reliable and from personal experience. Although the best effort was made by the author, there are no guarantees as to the accuracy or completeness of the contents within this work.

The author does not guarantee the accuracy of any information or content in resources or websites listed or cited within this work. Additionally, the author, publisher and distributors never give medical, legal, accounting or any other type of professional advice. The reader must always seek those services from competent professionals that can review the particular circumstances. Mention of any product, brand or website is NOT an endorsement or recommendation of that product, service or usage.

The medical field is a very dynamic field that is constantly undergoing research, modifications and advancements and therefore information contained in this book should always be researched further and A VETERINARIAN OR OTHER

SPECIALIST SHOULD BE CONSULTED where appropriate.

Any and all application of the information contained in this book is of the sole responsibility of the person performing said action. The author, publisher and distributors particularly disclaim any liability, loss, or risk taken by individuals who directly or indirectly act on the information herein. All readers must accept full responsibility for their use of this material.

Acknowledgements

The publisher thanks Danielle Shurskis for her support and help in bringing these series of books and articles to publication.

Cover

Photograph

© Gary Auerback | Dreamstime.com
Title "Mother Goat Nursing"

Cover Designer

Felicity McCullough

Publication Copyright 2012 ©

My Lap Shop Publishers

Table of Contents

Weaning Your Goat Kids Guide

Weaning

Weaning is when milk is removed from the kid's diet. It is a very important … and stressful … time for both the mother and the kid. If done right, weaning need not be overly stressful.

The most important factor is to make sure that the kid is already eating enough dry feed and forage, so that it won't feel the loss of the milk as much as a kid that is still only drinking milk, or mostly drinking milk. This is done with creep feeding.

You have several options including letting the mother decide when the kid is weaned, called natural weaning, or you can choose the date. If you choose to wean before the kid is 90 days of age, it is called Early Weaning. It is called Late Weaning if the kid is older than 90 days when weaned.

In this mini book, we will take a closer look at the details of weaning including, when to wean.

When to Wean

There are three basic ways to decide when to wean. Either you: (1) look at the calendar and use the kid's age, (2) use how much the kid weighs, or (3) let the mother and kid figure it out naturally without interference.

People wean anywhere from 14 days of age to six months or more, in the case of natural weaning. Kids that are artificially reared are normally weaned at six to eight weeks of age.

In essence, there is no best time to wean. Instead, you need to take a close look at your operation and production system and decide what is best for you.

Weaning Your Goat Kids Guide

There are advantages and disadvantages to every weaning systems and weaning ages.

When you are deciding when to wean, really take a close look at the kid. It will be the one to tell you the earliest that it can be weaned. Make sure that it is healthy, heavy enough and eating enough dry forage to sustain itself. You also have to take a close look at your operation and what is best for your business.

The kid should be about two to 2.5 times its birth weight and already eating a good amount of dry feed. A good amount means roughly 1% of its bodyweight. This amount should be enough to maintain its growth.

Age

It is generally agreed that it is actually better to wean based on the kid's size rather than its age. Kids should be weaned at least roughly twice to two and a half times the birth weight. This translates roughly to 20 to 25 pounds for both meat and dairy kids.

Season of Birth

When the kids are born is an important factor in weaning as well. Goats are naturally seasonal breeders, meaning that they enter into the breeding season when the light in the environment is diminishing; in other words, in the autumn and winter in the northern hemisphere.

The goat's gestation period is roughly five months. Kids will be born in late winter or spring, if they are bred in the autumn as is natural. This can be manipulated by the producer using artificial light and hormones. It is common to wean kids born in the winter early.

Parasites

You need to consider if weaning will hurt or help the parasite problem. Weaning causes stress in kids and dams. Stress can lead to a diminishing of the immune systems and allow parasites to flourish. This is especially true with worms and Coccidia.

Right around birth, dams naturally experience a dip in the immune system's protection that results in a worm population growth. Make sure to take this into consideration and evaluate the need for worm control and when planning weaning dates.

Predators

Having kids on the property, especially in winter, poses a threat of predators. If you have had a lot of losses from predators, consider weaning early in order to finish the kids earlier.

Market

Look at the market and see if you want to sell younger kids. If it is profitable, then you may want to wean early. If it isn't profitable, then perhaps you want to wait to hit another market.

Labour Available

Look at the amount of labour available. Do you have the time? Do you need to hire extra help? Artificially reared kids, for example, are usually weaned early to save labour, as well as the cost of milk replacer.

Facilities and Equipment Availability

The more you separate your herd into lots or groups for management, the more facilities and equipment you will need. Each group will need its own pen, which means more fencing, shelters, feeders and water containers etc.

Forage

Look at both the availability and quality of the forage that your goats have to eat. Weaning early is smart in a drought year, when forage is low quality and not enough is available, because you will better their nutrition by separating and supplementing them.

Preparing for Weaning

There are ways to diminish the stress of weaning. One is to make sure that you do not change the kid's diet the two weeks leading up to and the two weeks after weaning. Also, do not perform any vaccinations on the kids for the two weeks before weaning. Do not wean gradually. Abruptly taking the kid away from the milk and the doe is best.

Vaccination

The vaccination for CD-T should take place weeks before or after. Vaccinating before weaning is best so that the kids are ready for any challenge. Make sure to vaccinate more than two weeks before the planned weaning date.

The CD-T vaccine is to vaccinate against Overeating Disease, which is caused by *Clostridium perfringens* types C and D. The T stands for Tetanus, which is caused by *Clostridium tetani*.

It's recommended to apply the two doses of vaccine at roughly six and ten weeks of age, so you have a big window to work with when planning the management of your herd. If the dams of your kids were not vaccinated, then you will have to move the vaccination of the kids up to four and eight weeks of age.

If you disbud or castrated kids from does that weren't vaccinated, you will also need to administer the tetanus antitoxin. These practices are usually done within the first two weeks of age.

Coccidiosis

Coccidiosis is a common disease caused by a single-celled protozoa called Coccidia, which are located in the cells that make up the walls of the small intestines. Thus, the main symptom of Coccidiosis is diarrhoea. It causes reduced performance and death.

There are different species of Coccidia that can vary from non-infective to highly infective. Coccidia are species-specific, meaning that if a chicken has Coccidiosis on your property, it cannot transmit the disease to your goats. There are certain species that can infect both sheep and goats.

Coccidiosis prevention is important for kids, especially if they are raised indoors, or in confinement. Even animals raised on pasture can have confinement-like situations in such high-congregation areas as where the feeders and mineral mixes are kept. Any times when stress levels rise,

Coccidiosis tend to develop. Weaning time is one such example for kids.

It is impossible to eliminate Coccidia from a herd. Therefore, your goal should be population control and to make sure that the goats build up immunity to the protozoa so that even though the protozoa are present, they do not cause the disease.

There are products on the market that are called Coccidiostats or Ionophors and others that are used to treat the disease by killing the Coccidia. Coccidiostats / Ionophors diminish the growth of Coccidia. There are at least five products on the market that can be used with goats: Bovatec®,

Rumensin®, Deccox®, Albon and Amprolium.

Bovatec® is approved in the U.S. for sheep, Rumensin® is approved for goats and Deccox® is approved for both. Bovatec® and Rumensin® are administered mixed with the goat's food. Deccox® is mixed with loose trace mineral salt. Consult the label and or your veterinarian for dosages.

Two drugs that are used to treat Coccidia, which kill them, are Corid or Amprolium and Albon or Sulfadimethoxine. It is not approved for goats; therefore you will need a veterinarian to use it. It is not a coccidiostat; rather it is used as a treatment to kill the Coccidia. It is put in the drinking water for 21 days, or used as a drench. It needs 21 days to work because that is the full life cycle of the Coccidia and they have to be exposed through the cycle.

A word of caution, Rumensin® is highly toxic to all types of equines. To be on the safe side, you probably shouldn't administer any kind of coccidiostat if you have horses on the property.

Good sanitation is important to prevent Coccidiosis. Clean out the manure and even wash the facility, if possible. Lots of sunlight and keeping the area clean are the best disinfectants.

How to Wean

The first step is to decide when to wean. Then what? What exactly do you have to do to wean the kids?

It is best to wean abruptly rather than diluting the milk, or reducing feedings. On the day that you decide to wean, simply remove the does from the kids and do not give any more milk or milk replacer.

A tip is to make sure to wean the does from the kids and not the other way around. It is important for the kids to stay in familiar surroundings and to move the does into the new location separate from the kids, in order to minimise stress. Keep the group the same.

In fact, if you have a pasture that is right next to the one with the kids and that shares a fence line, it is even better because then the kids and moms can still see each other. They can have contact across the fence line.

Weaning Systems

There are three basic "systems" which are used to wean: natural weaning, early weaning, and late weaning. We will discuss these three systems below.

Natural Weaning

In natural weaning, you aren't really weaning at all. You simply let nature take its course, so to speak. You let the dam and kids sort it out between themselves. Usually this means that the mother will continue to feed the baby until she runs out of milk.

Early Weaning

Early weaning is the practice of removing milk from the diet in kids that are less than 90 days of age. Kids can range from 14 to 90 days of age, with above 60 days of age being the norm.

Advantages of this system include easing the stress on high-producing females. Animals that produce a lot of milk are under a lot of stress and weaning early, will lighten this stress. It will also help prolific females raise their offspring. Early weaning is often used in herds with a lot of triplets for this reason.

If the does are weaned earlier, they will dry off earlier and consequently, can be bred earlier. The risk of predators is lessened if kids are weaned earlier and sold to market, or prepared for breeding.

You also save on feeding costs since it is cheaper to feed just the kids instead of the dam and the offspring. Kids are much more efficient when converting feed for growth than does are at converting feed for lactation.

Some of the disadvantages include the stress that weaning puts on the dam and kid, a greater risk of mastitis in does that still have milk at the time of weaning and you will need more facilities and pastures because you are splitting up the herd. It also requires a higher degree of management on your part.

Early weaning is most commonly used in semi-intensive production systems and where kids are born in the winter, or raised indoors, as well as with prolific females, show does, creep feeding, and to finish kids on grain or grain and forage.

Dairy does are also normally early weaned so that the milk can be sold instead of used to raise the kids. Sometimes the kid is even removed after 24 hours and artificially reared.

Another option is to let the kid remain with the doe for about a month and then wean them.

Artificially-reared kids are normally weaned early as well, at six to eight weeks of age. This is often necessary because of the time, effort and cost of artificial rearing. Milk replacer is not cheap and neither is the cost of labour, even your labour.

Pasture is a limiting factor. In other words, if your pasture is not enough or low quality, you will early wean and supply supplemental feed.

Late Weaning

Late weaning is when you take the milk away from kids that are over 90 days of age. It is closer to natural weaning and therefore is less stressful to both the dams and the kids.

There is also less of a chance that the doe will develop Mastitis, because they are producing less milk. It depends on when you wean. For example, a doe at 90 days of lactation is producing much more milk than one at 150 days.

Late weaning allows you to take advantage of the forage that is available to finish the kids, which often is more economical than finishing on grain. It also makes management easier because the herd can be in one group.

The disadvantages of late weaning is that the kids are competing with the does for the forage available in the pasture and kids are more likely to become parasitized, because the does are depositing eggs that the kids are then exposed to. The risk of predators is higher. You may need to castrate or separate the males because they mature early.

Late weaning is most often used in semi-extensive production systems, in spring kidding, in systems where kidding happens in pasture and with less prolific does. It does not require creep feeding, although it is possible if so desired, and kids can be finished on pasture.

Creep Feeding

Creep feeding is the use of a space that is designed so that only kids can access it while the does remain outside. Inside this area there is a feeder where you put the special grain and forage for the kids.

The importance of offering kids grain and forage before weaning cannot be stressed enough. It is essential for many reasons. One of the most important is that it stimulates the proper development of the rumen.

Goats have four "stomachs": the reticulum, the rumen, the omasum and the abomasum. Each "stomach" has a different function in the digestion of the diet with the abomasum corresponding to the monogastric stomach. A monogastric animal is one with one stomach, like a horse, pig or even a human.

Although all parts of the gastric system is important and has its own function, arguably the most important part is the rumen. The rumen is full of microorganisms that break down the cellulose and other parts of the tough plants that form the ruminant diet. These are the parts that we and other monogastric animals cannot digest. The reason that ruminants can, is because of these microbes that are located in the rumen.

After the microbes are done with the feed, they produce what is called volatile fatty acids (VFA) which provide the goat with energy. These VFAs are absorbed through the rumen wall with something called papillae. These papillae develop faster in kids that are fed grain earlier. Papillae will form faster in kids that are fed forage than those fed just plain milk, yet the best results are with grain.

The faster development of papillae, and therefore the maturation of the rumen, is why creep feeding is so important. If you provide grain to the whole herd, the does will eat it all and the kids won't get any. There is always a danger for Overeating Disease if does have constant access, although this danger isn't present for kids, because their rumens aren't fully developed. Start creep feeding at roughly seven to ten days of life.

Creep Grazing

Creep feeding on pasture is called Creep Grazing. Creep grazing is where you separate a better quality pasture just for the kids.

Creep grazing is less commonly used when kids are raised on pasture, yet it is possible and it does have many advantages. For one, creep grazing improves the growth rate of kids. Consequently, you can get kids to market earlier. Better nutrition, especially higher protein, also means improved performance against parasites as well. There is also less contamination of this pasture from the does.

Whether or not you decide to Creep Graze depends on the economics of your farm, which species you are raising and even the kind of year you are having in terms of such things as pasture and rain fall. You will need to take a hard look at your farm to see if it is worth it.

How to Build It

Set up the creep feeder in high traffic areas and make sure that there are several openings and good visibility. The visibility is important because the kids need to see the does and vice versa if you want to make sure that the kids use the creep feeder. Make sure that it is kept clean, dry and with a nice, thick layer of bedding. The idea is to make this area enjoyable to be in.

When building or purchasing a feeder, make sure there is roughly two inches or five centimetres of space for each kid and that the pen has at least two square feet, or 0.19 square metres of space per kid.

Stocking the Feeder

You are probably wondering what to serve the kids in the creep feeder. The ration or grain that you purchase should have small particles and be easily digestible. Remember that their rumen isn't working correctly and they need something digestible. Make sure that it is fresh and palatable with high protein content.

Grain corn and Soybean meal are excellent choices. They love soybean meal at all ages. They like corn as they get older.

It is essential and cannot be stressed enough that this grain or ration needs to be available at all times. Kids do not tend to get Overeating Disease, as stated above, because their rumens aren't fully developed … unless the feeder runs out and is replenished. They will then gorge on the feed and likely die from Overeating Disease.

As they get older, it is important to balance this feed. When they are younger, it is more important that they simply eat some dry feed and it isn't as important to balance the diet.

Drying the Does

You must also plan on how you are going to dry your does. Drying does is important, because the tissues that make up the udder require this rest in order to prepare for the next cycle.

Remove the grain and protein of the ration one to two weeks prior to the date that you plan to wean. A few days before the planned weaning date also remove the good hay and switch to a low quality hay, or even straw until a few days after weaning.

Some people restrict water intake right before and right after weaning. Do not restrict water if the weather is too hot. Also keep an eye out for signs of Mastitis. These signs include an engorged, hot udder that is painful to the touch. It takes a month or two to completely dry off.

Resources

Schoenian, Susan. Weaning. 02/23/2011. Available at: - http://www.sheepandgoat.com/recordings.html.

Rook, J.S. Coccidiosis in Lambs. Michigan State University. Available at:- http://old.cvm.msu.edu/extension/Rook/ROOKpdf/coccidia.PDF.

Neary, Michael. Coccidiosis in Goats. Purdue University. November 2010. Available at: - http://www.ansc.purdue.edu/SP/MG/Coccidiosis.html.

Copyright 2012

My Lap Shop Publishers

All Rights Reserved.

Publishers

My Lap Shop Publishers

91 Mayflower Street, Unit 222,

Plymouth, Devon, PL1 1SB

United Kingdom

Tel: +44 (0)871 560 5297

www.mylapshop.com

www.goatlapshop.com

About My Lap Shop Publishers

First Edition September 2012

ISBN - 978-1-78165-043-1

About Felicity McCullough

Felicity McCullough has written several books about preventative health care for goats. The website dedicated to goats www.goatlapshop.com has a wide variety of topics and resources that relate to goats, including the Charlie And Isabella's Magical Adventures Series of Children's Books, suitable for bed-time reading that are beautifully illustrated.

Goat Knowledge Series Titles

How To Keep Goats Healthy #1
ISBN: 978-1-78165-021-9

Golden Guernsey Goats #2
ISBN: 978-1-78165-022-6

A Simple Guide To The Goat's
Digestive System #3
ISBN: 978-1-78165-024-0

Success Guide For Raising Healthy
Goats #4
ISBN: 978-1-78165-026-4

Managing Goat Nutrition: What You
Need To Know A Simple Guide #5
ISBN: 978-1-78165-027-1

Plants And Goats An Easy To Read
Guide #6
ISBN: 978-1-78165-038-7

Goat Housing, Bedding, Fencing,
Exercise Yards And Pasture
Management Guide #7
ISBN: 978-1-78165-040-0

Other Goat Books and Articles

by Felicity McCullough

www.goatlapshop.com

Boar Goats

Charlie And Isabella's Magical Adventure

Charlie And Isabella Meet Jacob

Charlie And Isabella's Second Adventure With Jacob

Charlie And Isabella's Magical Adventures Compendium

Diseases of Goats

Goat Basics

Goat Breed: Golden Guernsey Goats

Goat Videos

How To Keep Goats Healthy

Nigerian Dwarf Goats

Nimbkar Boer Goat

Weaning Your Goat Kids Guide

Raising Goats Easy Guide To Raising
and Caring for Goats
The Fun of Goats

My Lap Shop Publishers
Plymouth, England
www.mylapshop.com